Key Differences Between National Bank Regulatory Requirements
and Federal Savings Association Regulatory Requirements

Table of Contents

FOREWORD

This document is designed to provide guidance to assist in understanding the OCC's authority to supervise both national banks and federal savings associations. It is not meant to provide a comprehensive analysis of all the regulations or policies applicable to or the powers of these institutions, but rather to provide a brief guide to some of the key differences. The guide contains references to relevant statutes and regulations, including OTS regulations reissued as part of the Code of Federal Regulations codified at 12 CFR 100-199.

Over time, the OCC will be consolidating and harmonizing the separate rules and policies, so these materials are meant to provide guidance on some of the key differences that currently exist. Finally, you may wish to consult the document entitled *Comparison Of The Powers Of National Banks And Federal Savings Associations*.

This document was prepared by the OCC's Chief Counsel's Office. It is not intended to provide official legal interpretations and does not create any rights or obligations of third parties.

Key Differences between
National Bank Regulatory Requirements and Federal Savings Association Regulatory Requirements

I. GENERAL POWERS AND OPERATIONAL REQUIREMENTS

Lending/Investment Powers

Federal savings associations and national banks have different lending and investment powers. The chart below lists a few of those differences. The chart is not all inclusive nor does it contain all the qualifications and conditions which may place additional limitations on these lending and investment powers. For additional information on savings association lending and investment powers, please refer to 12 U.S.C. § 1464(c) and 12 C.F.R. Part 160. For additional information on national bank lending and investment powers, please refer to 12 U.S.C. §§ 24(Seventh), 24(Eleventh), and 371. Another useful source is the document entitled "Comparison of the Powers of National Banks and Federal Savings Associations."

The chart below contains limits on loan/investment categories as a percentage of capital or assets.[1]

Category	Federal Savings Assn Limit	National Bank Limit
Asset-Backed Securities	No limit for mortgage-backed securities. For other asset-backed securities, aggregate limit and eligibility to invest depend upon the type of asset that is securitized. Certain securities will be subject to credit risk retention.	No limit for mortgage-backed securities that qualify as certain Type IV securities. Other asset-backed securities that qualify as Type V securities have per issuer limit of 25% of bank's capital and surplus.
Commercial loans	20% of total assets, provided that amounts in excess of 10% of total assets may be used only for small business loans. Exceptions for certain loans to insured financial institutions, brokers, and dealers.	No limit.

---

[1] Additional limitations may be applicable under the statutes and regulations, which the reader is urged to consult.

Category	Federal Savings Assn Limit	National Bank Limit
Commercial paper and corporate debt securities	35% of total assets, combined with consumer loans. Per issuer limit of 10% of unimpaired capital and surplus.	Per issuer limit of 10% of capital and surplus for a Type III security. Generally, aggregated with Type II securities of the same issuer.
Community development loans and equity investments	If pursuant to 42 U.S.C. § 5301 et seq., aggregate limit of 5% of total assets. Equity investments must not exceed 2% of total assets. If type of investment permitted for national bank under 12 C.F.R. Part 24, aggregate limit of greater of 1% of total capital or $250,000.	Aggregate investment limit is 5% of capital and surplus, but may invest up to 15% of capital and surplus with OCC approval.
Construction loans without security	Aggregate limit of the greater of total capital or 5% of total assets.	No limit.
Consumer loans	Aggregate limit of 35% of total assets, combined with commercial paper and corporate debt securities.	No limit.
Nonconforming loans, secured primarily by residential or farm real property	5% of total assets.	No limit.
Nonresidential real property loans	400% of total capital.	No limit.
Service corporations	3% of total assets, as long as any amounts in excess of 2% of total assets further community, inner city, or community development purposes.	N/A[2]

---

[2] But see later discussion regarding subsidiaries and noncontrolling investments.

Category	Federal Savings Assn Limit	National Bank Limit
Small business investment companies	5% of total capital.	5% of capital and surplus.
Small business-related securities	None, provided securities rated in 1 of 4 highest rating categories that represent an interest in promissory notes or leases of personal property evidencing obligations of small business concern.	None, provided securities are fully secured by interests in a pool of loans to numerous obligors and securities are rated investment grade in the highest two investment grade rating categories.
State and local government obligations	None for general obligations. Per issuer limitation of 10% of capital for other obligations – see 12 C.F.R. § 160.42 for further detail.	None, for general obligations of state and local governments that are Type I securities. Well-capitalized banks may invest in revenue bonds without limit. Per issuer limit of 10% of capital and surplus if a Type II security.

Nonresidential Real Property Loans - 12 U.S.C. § 1464(c)(2)(B)

As indicated in the chart above, a federal savings association's aggregate amount of loans secured by liens on nonresidential real property generally cannot exceed 400% of total capital. However, the statute provides that the OCC may permit a federal savings association to exceed the 400% limitation if the OCC determines that the increased authority poses no significant risk to the safe and sound operation of the association and is consistent with prudent operating practices.

A federal savings association seeking to exceed the 400% limit must file an application with its appropriate Licensing office. There is no specific form for this filing, but the application should address the information discussed in OTS Applications Handbook, Section 830. Licensing will seek the supervisory office's recommendation on the application. See OTS Applications Handbook, Section 830 for decision guidelines to consider when reviewing the application.

General Lending Limit/Loans to One Borrower ("LTOB") - 12 C.F.R. Part 32 and 12 C.F.R. § 160.93(d)

Generally, federal savings associations and national banks are subject to the same general lending limits (see 12 C.F.R. Part 32 for national banks and 12 C.F.R. § 160.93 for savings associations). However, there are two additional provisions that are applicable only to federal savings associations (see 12 C.F.R. § 160.93(d)).

- If a federal savings association's aggregate lending limitation is less than $500,000, such savings association may have total loans and extensions of credit, for any purpose, to one borrower outstanding at one time not to exceed $500,000.
- A federal savings association may make loans to one borrower to develop domestic residential housing units, not to exceed the lesser of $30,000,000 or 30% of the savings association's unimpaired capital and unimpaired surplus, including all amounts loaned under the general lending limit, provided that:

> (i) The final purchase price of each single family dwelling unit the development of which is financed under this paragraph does not exceed $500,000;
>
> (ii) The savings association is, and continues to be, in compliance with its capital requirements;
>
> (iii) The OCC permits the savings association to use the higher limit (subject to any conditions imposed by the OCC); [3]
>
> (iv) Loans made pursuant to this provision to all borrowers do not, in aggregate, exceed 150% of the savings association's unimpaired capital and unimpaired surplus; and
>
> (v) Such loans comply with the applicable loan-to-value requirements that apply to federal savings associations.

---

[3] A federal savings association that meets the requirements of the regulation, and is eligible for "expedited treatment" under 12 C.F.R. § 116.5 may use the higher limit if the association has filed a notice with OCC that it intends to use the higher limit at least *30 days* prior to the proposed use. A savings association that meets the requirements of the regulation, and is subject to "standard treatment" under 12 C.F.R. § 116.5 may use the higher limit if the savings association has filed an application with OCC and OCC has approved the use of the higher limit. Approval of notices and applications will generally provide blanket approval to the association to exceed the lending limitations with all borrowers for the purpose of loans to develop residential housing units, subject to the aggregate limit of 150% of unimpaired capital and surplus. However, OCC may determine that a filing is required for each borrower in circumstances when safety and soundness concerns exist.

To be eligible for expedited treatment, a federal savings association must meet the following requirements: (i) has a composite rating of "1" or "2"; (ii) has a CRA rating of "Satisfactory" or "Outstanding"; (iii) has a compliance rating of "1" or "2"; (iv) complies with all capital requirements under 12 C.F.R. Part 167; and (iv) has not been notified by its regulator that it is in "troubled condition." A savings association is subject to "standard treatment" if it meets any of the following criteria: (i) has a composite rating of "3", "4", or "5"; (ii) has a CRA rating of "Needs to Improve" or "Substantial Noncompliance"; (iii) has a compliance rating of "3", "4", or "5"; (iv) does not comply with all capital requirements under 12 C.F.R. Part 167; or (iv) has been notified by its regulator that it is in "troubled condition."

The authority of a federal savings association to make a loan or extension of credit under this provision ceases immediately upon the association's failure to comply with any one of the requirements set forth in the regulation or any conditions imposed by the OCC under (iii) above.

As indicated in footnote 3, a federal savings association must file either a notice or application with the supervisory office before using the higher limit authority for domestic residential housing unit development. *For notices, the supervisory office must act within 30 calendar days of the notice filing date. For applications, the supervisory office must act within 60 calendar days of the date the application is deemed complete. If the supervisory office fails to act within the required time frames, the notice or application is deemed to be automatically approved.* See OTS Applications Handbook, Section 820, for more information on notice/application requirements and processing timeframes.

Additional Lending Limit for Residential Real Estate Loans, Small Business Loans, and Small Farm Loans - 12 C.F.R. §§ 32.7 and 160.93

Generally, these limits are the same for national banks and federal savings associations. Banks and savings associations that want to use the higher limits must file an application with the supervisory office. OCC has internal guidelines for processing these applications for national banks. Guidelines for processing these applications for savings associations may be found at OTS Applications Handbook, Section 850.

Although the approval standards are similar for both banks and federal savings associations, there are two additional items you should consider when reviewing an application from a federal savings association:

- Will the savings association maintain compliance with the limitations set forth in 12 U.S.C. § 1464(c)(2)(A) and 12 C.F.R. § 160.30 with respect to small business loans?
- How will the increase in this type of lending affect the savings association's Qualified Thrift Lender (QTL) status? (An exception will not be granted if the savings association will fail its QTL test as a result of the increase in nonresidential real property lending.)

There is an important difference in how these applications are processed for federal savings associations and national banks, which is described below.

Federal Savings Associations

The OCC must notify the federal savings association of OCC's receipt of the application within *5 business days*. *The application will be automatically approved upon the expiration of 30 calendar days after the filing of the application, unless OCC takes one of the following actions before expiration of the 30 days*:

- Requests, in writing, any additional information necessary to supplement the application;
- Notifies the savings association that the application raises a supervisory concern, raises a significant issue of law or policy, or requires significant additional information; or
- Denies the application.

If supplemental information is requested, the savings association has *30 calendar days* to provide such information. The 30-day application review period will restart upon receipt of such information.

National Banks

Applications filed by national banks are not subject to the 30 day automatic approval requirement.

Qualified Thrift Lender - 12 U.S.C. § 1467a(m)

Federal Savings Associations

A federal savings association is required to be a qualified thrift lender ("QTL").[4] To be a QTL, an association must meet either the Home Owners' Loan Act Qualified Thrift Lender Test ("QTL Test") (12 U.S.C. § 1467a(m)) or the Internal Revenue Service tax code Domestic Building and Loan Association Test ("DBLA Test") (26 C.F.R. § 301.7701-13A).

Under the QTL Test, an association must hold qualified thrift investments[5] equal to at least 65% of its portfolio assets (see OTS Examination Handbook, Section 270, for definition of "qualified thrift investment" and "portfolio assets"). An association ceases to be a QTL when its ratio of qualified thrift investments (numerator) divided by its

---

[4] A federal savings association that fails to become or remain a qualified thrift lender is deemed to have violated section 5 of the HOLA and may be subject to enforcement action. See, 12 U.S.C. § 1467a(m)(3)(B)(i)(IV).

[5] Qualified thrift investments include loans to purchase, refinance, construct, improve, or repair domestic residential or manufactured housing; home equity loans; educational loans; small business loans; loans made through credit cards or credit card accounts; securities backed by or representing an interest in mortgages on domestic residential or manufactured housing; and FHLB stock. For a complete list, see 12 U.S.C. § 1467a(m)(4)(C).

portfolio assets (denominator) falls, at month-end, below 65% for four months within any 12 month period.

Under the DBLA Test, an association must meet a "business operations test" and a "60% of assets test."

- The "business operations test" requires the business of a DBLA to consist primarily of acquiring the savings of the public and investing in loans (see OTS Examination Handbook, Section 270, for more information on public savings requirement and investing in loans requirement).
- The "60% of assets test" requires that at least 60% of a DBLA's assets must consist of assets that associations normally hold, except for consumer loans that are not educational loans.

A federal savings association may use either the QTL test or the DBLA test to qualify as a QTL and may switch from one test to the other (see OTS Examination Handbook, Section 270, for more information).

Except as provided below, a federal savings association that fails to become or remain a QTL is subject to the following restrictions:

- Restrictions effective immediately
  - Shall not make any new investments or engage in any new activity not allowed for both a national bank and a savings association;
  - Shall not establish any new branch office unless allowable for a national bank; and
  - Shall not pay dividends unless: (i) allowable for a national bank; (ii) necessary to meet obligations of a company that controls the federal savings association; and (iii) the dividend receives OCC and Federal Reserve Board approval.
- Additional restrictions effective after three years
  - If an association fails to requalify as a QTL within 3 years, the association must dispose of or not engage in any activity unless the investment or activity is allowed for both a national bank and a savings association.

The restrictions listed above are not applicable if the association requalifies as a QTL. However, a savings association may requalify as a QTL only once. Failure to maintain QTL status after requalification permanently subjects a savings association to the restrictions described above.

The OCC may grant temporary and limited exceptions from compliance with the QTL test when extraordinary circumstances exist,[6] or to significantly facilitate an acquisition

---

[6] An example of an extraordinary circumstance is when the effects of high interest rates reduce mortgage demand to such a degree that an insufficient opportunity exists for an association to meet the QTL requirement. See 12 U.S.C. § 1467a(m)(2)(A). Also, OCC may facilitate an association's efforts to assist

of a troubled institution under 12 U.S.C. § 1823(c) or (k) (see OTS Examination Handbook, Section 270, for more information). A federal savings association requesting an exception from the QTL test must file a request with Licensing.

National Banks

A national bank is not required to be a qualified thrift lender.

Dividends/Capital Distributions

Federal savings associations and national banks are subject to different rules regarding dividends and capital distributions.

Federal Savings Associations - 12 C.F.R. §§ 163.140 - 163.146

When Application is Required

If a federal savings association meets any of the following criteria, it must file an application with the supervisory office *at least 30 days before* the proposed declaration of dividend or approval of the proposed capital distribution by the board of directors:

- Not eligible for expedited treatment under 12 C.F.R § 116.5.[7]
- Total amount of all capital distributions (including the proposed capital distribution) for the applicable calendar year exceeds the saving association's net income for that year to date plus retained net income for the preceding two years.
- Association would not be at least adequately capitalized, as set forth at 12 C.F.R. § 165.4(b)(2), following the distribution.[8]
- Proposed capital distribution would violate a prohibition contained in any applicable statute, regulation, or agreement between the savings association and OCC, or violate a condition imposed on the savings association in an OCC approved application or notice.

The OCC must notify the savings association of OCC's receipt of the application within *5 business days*. OCC has *30 calendar days* to review application to determine if application is complete, if additional information is needed, or decline to further process the application if it is deemed by OCC to be materially deficient or substantially incomplete. See OTS Applications Handbook, Section 635 for additional information on processing times if additional information is requested. Once the application is deemed complete, there is a *60 calendar day* review period during which time OCC will take into

---

communities affected by a natural disaster by temporarily waiving the QTL requirement to allow a capital compliant association to help rebuild non-QTL businesses. See Thrift Bulletin 71.

[7] See footnote 3 for explanation of "expedited treatment."

[8] But see 12 U.S.C. § 1831o(d)(1)(A) which provides that a savings association may not declare or pay any dividend, if, after making the dividend, the savings association would be "undercapitalized" as defined in 12 C.F.R. Part 167.

consideration all factors present in the application and render a decision. *If, upon expiration of the 60 calendar day review period, OCC has failed to act, the application is deemed approved.*

When Notice is Required

If a federal savings association meets any of the following criteria, and is not required to file an application as described above, it must file a notice with the supervisory office *at least 30 days* before the proposed declaration of dividend or approval of the proposed capital distribution by the board of directors:

- The savings association would not be well-capitalized, as defined at 12 C.F.R. § 165.4(b)(1), following the distribution.
- The proposed capital distribution would reduce the amount of or retire any part of the savings association's common or preferred stock or retire any part of debt instruments, such as notes or debentures included in capital under 12 C.F.R. Part 167 (other than regular payments required under a debt instrument approved under 12 C.F.R. § 163.81).
- The savings association is a subsidiary of a savings and loan holding company. However, where a savings association subsidiary of a stock savings and loan holding company is proposing to pay a cash dividend, only an informational filing is required - see discussion below.

Failure by the OCC to act within 30 calendar days of receipt of the notice for processing shall result in the notice being deemed approved.

When an Informational Submission is Required

Section 10(f) of the HOLA, 12 U.S.C. § 1467a(f), requires federal savings associations that are subsidiaries of savings and loan holding companies to file a notice of a proposed dividend with the FRB. This notice is separate from any notice or application required by the OCC's capital distribution regulations. If the savings association is not otherwise required to file an application or notice with the OCC, but is required to file a notice with the FRB under section 10(f) of the HOLA, 12 C.F.R. § 163.143(d) requires that the savings association provide an informational copy of the notice to its OCC supervisory office at the same time it is filed with the FRB.[9] The OCC has required that the association file the informational copy in order to assist the OCC in responding to requests from the FRB to comment on such filings. The FRB has stated that it intends to seek comment from the supervisory office regarding filings under section 10(f), and that it intends to request the supervisory office's comments within *15 days of receipt* of the FRB's request.

---

[9] This informational filing requirement applies only when a savings association subsidiary of a stock savings and loan holding company is proposing to pay a cash dividend. If the savings association is an indirect subsidiary of a mutual holding company, it is not eligible for the informational filing.

Although no formal OCC action is necessary with respect to the information submissions, it is expected that the supervisory office will comment to the FRB regarding these submissions within the requested period. The submissions should be evaluated under the same standards that apply to OCC review of capital distribution applications and notices.

<u>When No Filing is Required</u>

If a federal savings association does not meet any of the criteria listed above, it does not need to file a notice or application before making a capital distribution.

See <u>12 C.F.R. § 163.141</u> for the definition of "capital distribution"; <u>12 C.F.R. § 163.144</u> for the required contents of the notice or application; and <u>12 C.F.R. § 163.146</u> for factors the OCC will consider in reviewing the application or notice. The notice or application may include a schedule proposing capital distributions over a specified period not to exceed 12 months.

National Banks

<u>Dividends</u> - <u>12 U.S.C. §§ 56</u> and <u>60(b)</u>, <u>12 C.F.R. § 5.64</u>

Directors of a national bank may declare and pay dividends of so much of the undivided profits as they judge to be expedient, subject to the following restrictions:

- Unless approved by the OCC, a national bank may not declare a dividend if the total amount of all dividends (common and preferred), including the proposed dividend, declared by the national bank in any current year exceeds the total of the national bank's net income of the current year to date, combined with the retained net income of current year minus one and current year minus two, less the sum of any transfers required by the OCC and any transfers required to be made to a fund for the retirement of any preferred stock.[10] See <u>12 U.S.C. § 60(b)</u> and <u>12 C.F.R. § 5.64(c)(2)</u>.
  - Requests for prior approval of a dividend under <u>12 U.S.C. § 60(b)</u> are submitted to the supervisory office. There is no specified time frame by which the notice must be filed; however, the board cannot declare the dividend until it receives OCC approval. See <u>OCC Licensing Manual, Capital and Dividends Book</u>let, for information that must be included in national bank's incoming request and factors the OCC will consider in reviewing the notice.
- If a national bank has sustained losses at any time that equal or exceed its undivided profits (a/k/a retained earnings), then the bank is prohibited from paying a dividend. See <u>12 U.S.C. § 56</u>. However, this rule does not prevent the bank from making a reduction of permanent capital pursuant to <u>12 U.S.C. § 59</u> (see discussion below).

---

[10] This requirement is essentially the same as one of the criteria triggering application for savings associations.

- A national bank may not declare or pay any dividend if, after making the dividend, that national bank would be "undercapitalized" as defined in 12 C.F.R Part 6. See 12 U.S.C. § 1831o(d)(1)(A).

<u>Reduction in Permanent Capital</u> - 12 U.S.C. § 59 and 12 C.F.R. § 5.46

In addition to dividends, a national bank has the option of reducing permanent capital. See 12 U.S.C. § 59 and 12 C.F.R. § 5.46. "Permanent capital" is defined as the sum of capital stock and capital surplus. "Capital surplus" is defined as the total of: (i) the amount paid in on capital stock in excess of the par or stated value; (ii) direct capital contributions representing the amounts paid in to the national bank other than for capital stock; (iii) the amount transferred from undivided profits; and (iv) the amount transferred from undivided profits reflecting stock dividends.

- A national bank must obtain the necessary shareholder approval required by statute for any change in its permanent capital.
- A national bank must submit an application to Licensing and obtain prior OCC approval for any reduction of its permanent capital. The application must contain the information required by 12 C.F.R. § 5.46(i)(1).

Investment in Bank Premises

Federal savings associations and national banks are subject to different rules regarding investment in bank premises.

Federal Savings Associations - 12 C.F.R. § 160.37

Under 12 C.F.R. § 160.37, a federal savings association may not make an investment in bank premises that would cause the outstanding book value of all such investments to exceed total capital.

A federal savings association may request a waiver of this investment limit by filing a waiver application (in letter form) with the supervisory office. See OTS Applications Handbook, Section 840, for decision guidelines and processing timeframes. Please note that once the application is deemed complete, OCC has a *60 calendar day* review period. *If the OCC fails to act within that 60-day time period, the application is deemed automatically approved*.

National Banks - 12 U.S.C. § 371(d); 12 C.F.R. § 7.1000(c); 12 C.F.R. § 5.37

Except as noted below, a national bank must obtain OCC approval to make an investment in bank premises that exceeds the capital stock of the bank. The application process is detailed at 12 C.F.R. § 5.37(d). *The application is filed with the supervisory office and is deemed approved as of the 30th day after the filing is received by the OCC, unless the*

OCC notifies the bank prior to that date that the filing presents a significant supervisory, or compliance concern, or raises a significant legal or policy issue.

A national bank that has a composite rating of "1" or "2" may make an aggregate investment in bank premises up to 150% of the bank's capital and surplus without OCC's prior approval, provided that the bank is "well capitalized" and will continue to be well capitalized after the investment or loan is made. The bank shall notify the supervisory office in writing of the investment *within 30 days* after the investment or loan is made. The written notice must include a description of the bank's investment.

REO/OREO

Federal savings associations are subject to a regulation regarding the holding period for real estate owned ("REO"), but have no regulations regarding the disposition of REO or additional expenditures on REO – these issues are addressed by policy. By comparison, national banks are subject to regulations regarding the holding period for other real estate owned ("OREO") disposition of OREO, and additional expenditures on OREO.

Federal Savings Associations - 12 C.F.R. § 167.1

The REO holding period for savings associations is found in the capital regulations. Generally, a savings association must deduct equity investments in real property from total assets and total capital. However, there is an exception to this rule that provides that REO is not considered an equity investment in real property (and thus does not need to be deducted from capital), provided that the property is not intended to be held for real estate investment purposes but is expected to be disposed of within 5 years unless a longer period is approved by the OCC. See 12 C.F.R. § 167.1. A savings association that wants an extension of the 5-year holding period must file a request with, and receive approval from, the supervisory office. See OTS Examination Handbook, Section 251, for further detail.

With the exception of the 5 year holding period, there is no other regulatory requirement governing a savings association's disposition of REO. However, OTS Examination Handbook, Section 251, provides that once a savings association acquires a property through foreclosure or repossession, management should begin the decision making process of whether to hold the property or sell it. See OTS Examination Handbook, Section 251.

There is also no regulation governing a savings association's additional expenditures on REO. However, OTS Examination Handbook, Section 211, indicates that salvage powers have provided legal justification for a savings association to hold, operate (if necessary), and invest additional funds (when necessary) in property acquired as result of, or in lieu of, foreclosure prior to resale of the property. The OTS took the position that an association has inherent or implied authority to take whatever steps may be necessary to salvage an investment, provided that the steps taken: (i) are an integral part of a reasonable and *bona fide* salvage plan; and (ii) do not contravene a specific legal prohibition (OTS did not consider the lending limit to be a specific legal prohibition within the meaning of the salvage powers doctrine). Accordingly, a savings association may use its salvage powers to exceed the lending limit provided it is able to demonstrate that it is making the excess investment pursuant to a reasonable and *bona fide* salvage plan. Excess investments that are not made pursuant to such a plan are illegal and could trigger possible enforcement action. ***A savings association that intends to make a salvage powers investment in excess of its lending limit must file a request with, and receive nonobjection from, the supervisory office.*** The supervisory office will take into consideration the risks posed by a proposed salvage plan, an association's past history of salvage operations, and the financial condition of the association and its ability to undertake the risks attendant to salvage operations. When reviewing a proposed salvage plan, the supervisory office will consider whether the plan meets the following criteria:

- is it necessary to enable the association to salvage its existing investment?
- is it necessary to protect the value of the foreclosed property (e.g., the additional investments will result in a more marketable property)?
- is it in the best interest of the association?
- will it reduce the risks associated with the foreclosed property?

See OTS Examination Handbook, Section 211, for additional information on salvage powers.

National Banks - 12 C.F.R. §§ 34.82, 34.83 and 34.86

Twelve C.F.R § 34.82 provides that a national bank shall dispose of OREO at the earliest time that prudent judgment dictates, but no later than 5 years (with a possible extension of up to an additional 5 years). See 12 U.S.C. § 29 for information on holding period. A national bank that wants an extension of the 5-year holding period must file a request with, and receive approval from, the supervisory office.

Twelve C.F.R. § 34.83 describes what transactions qualify as a disposition of OREO and requires that a national bank shall make diligent and ongoing efforts to dispose of each parcel of OREO, and shall maintain documentation adequate to reflect those efforts.

Twelve C.F.R. § 34.86 describes the process by which a national bank may make additional advances to complete an OREO project that is a development or improvement project. The regulation specifies that a national bank shall notify the supervisory office ***30 days before*** implementing a development or improvement plan for OREO when the sum of the plan's estimated cost and the bank's current recorded investment amount (including any unpaid prior liens) exceeds 10% of the bank's capital and surplus. The required notification must demonstrate that the additional expenditure is consistent with the conditions and limitations set forth at 12 C.F.R. § 34.86(a). The OCC has ***30 days*** to review the notice. ***Unless otherwise informed by the OCC, the bank may implement the plan on the 31*** st ***day (or sooner if notified by the OCC), subject to any conditions imposed by the OCC.***

Real Estate Development

Under certain circumstances, a service corporation of a federal savings association is permitted to hold real estate for investment and engage in real estate development. The activity is subject to the limitations of 12 C.F.R. § 159.5. The term "real estate development" refers to the development of land or other real estate for sale or lease in which the related organization has an ownership (equity) interest or actively manages the property. (Real estate owned, repossessed assets, and real estate held for use by a savings association or its subsidiary are not included in the definition of real estate development.)

A federal savings association's investment in (and loans to) a service corporation that engages in real estate development must be excluded from total assets and regulatory capital. See 12 U.S.C. § 1464(t)(5).

In contrast, national banks generally are not permitted to engage in real estate development. (But see OCC precedent for full utilization of property acquired for bank premises or to recover full value of OREO.)

Asset Classification - 12 C.F.R. § 160.160

Federal savings associations are subject to a regulation governing asset classification; there is no similar regulation for national banks.

Twelve C.F.R. § 160.160 provides that each savings association must evaluate and classify its assets on a regular basis in a manner consistent with, or reconcilable to, the asset classification system used by the OCC. If, during an examination, the examiners classify problem assets, the savings association must recognize such examiner classifications in subsequent reports to OCC. Based on the evaluation and classification of its assets, each savings association shall establish adequate valuation allowance or charge-offs, as appropriate, consistent with GAAP and the practices of the federal banking agencies.

For national banks, the classification of problem assets and the adequacy of valuation allowances are governed by guidance rather than by regulation. Depending on the circumstances, risk rating inaccuracies or an inadequate valuation allowance may be an unsafe or unsound practice.

Interest-Rate Risk Management Procedures - 12 C.F.R. § 163.176

Federal savings associations are subject to a regulation governing interest-rate risk management procedures; there is no similar regulation for national banks. Interagency guidance exists on this subject that is applicable to both national banks and federal savings associations: see Appendix A to 12 C.F.R. Part 30 (national banks) and Appendix A to 12 C.F.R. Part 170 (federal savings associations).

Twelve C.F.R. § 163.176 provides that savings associations shall take the following actions:

- The board of directors (Board) or a committee of the Board shall review the savings association's interest-rate risk exposure and devise a policy for the association's management of that risk.
- The Board shall adopt a formal policy for the management of interest-rate risk. The management shall establish guidelines and procedures to ensure that the Board's policy is successfully implemented.
- Management shall periodically report to the Board regarding implementation of the association's policy for interest-rate risk management and shall make that information available upon request of the OCC.
- The Board shall review the results of operations at least quarterly and shall make such adjustments as it considers necessary and appropriate to the policy for interest-rate risk management, including adjustments to the authorized acceptable level of interest-rate risk.

For national banks, interest-rate risk management issues are addressed through a safety and soundness analysis. Depending on the circumstances, weaknesses or deficiencies in interest-rate risk management procedures may be an unsafe or unsound practice.

Federal Reserve Bank/Federal Home Loan Bank Membership - 12 U.S.C. §§ 222, 1424, and 1464(f).

Federal savings associations and national banks are subject to different rules regarding membership in the Federal Reserve System but similar rules regarding membership in the Federal Home Loan Bank System.

A federal savings association is not required to be a member bank of the Federal Reserve System. By contrast, 12 U.S.C. § 222 requires national banks to be Federal Reserve System member banks.

Federal savings associations and national banks may be members of the Federal Home Loan Bank System, but they are not required to be members.

Business Plan Modifications for Federal Savings Associations and Banks

Federal Savings Associations - OTS Applications Handbook, Section 630

In some instances, a federal savings association may have been required to file a 3-year business plan in connection with certain applications, such as change in control and permission to organize applications. When OTS approved these applications, it generally imposed a standard condition that requires a savings association to obtain prior nonobjection from the OTS Regional Director for any material change in the business plan during the first 3 years.

Post-integration, these applications for business plan modifications will be filed with the supervisory office. Within *5 days of receipt* of the application, the ADC must notify the applicant of the application's receipt. Once the application is deemed complete, the OCC has *60 calendar days* to act on the application. *If the OCC does not act within the 60-day review period, non-objection is deemed to have been granted automatically and the federal savings association may implement the business plan modification.* See OTS Applications Handbook, Section 630 for information that must be included in the application and regulatory criteria and decision guidelines.

Applications are not required for certain business plan modifications, such as minor deviations from approved business plan that will not significantly alter the financial projections submitted with the approved business plan. See OTS Applications Handbook, Section 630 for other examples of when an association does not need to file an application for a business plan modification. It is within the ADC's discretion whether to accept the institution's justification that the deviation from the approved business plan is not material and requires no application, or make a determination that the deviation is material and requires an application.

National Banks - Comptroller's Licensing Manual, Charters, Appendix G

When OCC charters a new national bank, it imposes a standard condition in the approval letter that requires the national bank to provide prior notice and obtain a no objection letter from the appropriate supervisory office before making a significant deviation from its business plan for the first 3 years of operation (see Comptroller's Licensing Manual, Charters, Appendix G for explanation of the term "significant deviation."). Upon receipt of prior notice, the supervisory office will evaluate the proposed deviation. If the evaluation results in little or no supervisory concern, the supervisory office should send a no objection letter. If the evaluation discloses supervisory concerns, the supervisory office sends an "objection" letter detailing the reasons for this determination. *There is no required timeframe by which the supervisory office must act.*

Transactional Web Site - 12 C.F.R. §§ 155.300 and 155.310

Federal savings associations are subject to a regulation governing transactional web sites There is no similar regulation for national banks.

Twelve C.F.R. § 155.300 provides that all *savings associations must file a written notice with the supervisory office at least 30 days before establishing a transactional web site*. A transactional web site is an Internet site that enables users to conduct financial transactions such as accessing an account, obtaining an account balance, transferring funds, processing bill payments, opening an account, applying for or obtaining a loan, or purchasing other authorized products or services.

The notice must contain the following information:

- A description of the transactional web site.
- The date the transactional web site will become operational.
- A contact familiar with the deployment, operations, and security of the transactional web site.

II. INSIDER ISSUES

Changes In Director and Senior Executive Officers (Section 914 of FIRREA) - 12 C.F.R. §§ 5.51 and 163.550

Generally the regulations governing changes in directors and senior executive officers are the same for national banks and federal savings associations, but there are different prior notice and processing time requirements.

- The rule applicable to savings associations requires the savings association to file a notice with the supervisory office *30 days prior* to a change in directors or senior executive officers whereas the rule applicable to national banks requires the national bank to file a notice with the supervisory office *90 days prior* to the change.
- The savings association rule has a *30-day review requirement*, with permissible extensions for *up to 60 days*, whereas the national bank rule has a *90-day review period*.

Regulation O and Regulation W

Both national banks and federal savings associations are subject to the requirements of 12 U.S.C. §§ 375a and 375b, and 12 C.F.R. Part 215 (Regulation O).[11]

Both national banks and federal savings associations are subject to the requirements of 12 U.S.C. §§ 371c and 371c-1 and 12 C.F.R. Part 223 (Regulation W).[12] However, savings associations are subject to the following additional restrictions when engaging in transactions with affiliates:

- an association is prohibited from making a loan or extension of credit to an affiliate, unless the affiliate is engaged only in activities that the Board of

---

[11] See 12 U.S.C. § 1468(b) which provides that 12 U.S.C. §§ 375a and 375b shall apply to every savings association in the same manner and to the same extent as if the savings association were a member bank.

[12] See 12 U.S.C. § 1468(a) which generally provides that 12 U.S.C. §§ 371c and 371c-1 shall apply to every savings association in the same manner and to the same extent as if the savings association were a member bank, but adds the two additional restrictions listed in the main text above.

Governors of the Federal Reserve System, by regulation, has determined to be permissible for bank holding companies under 12 U.S.C. § 1843(c); and

- an association is prohibited from purchasing or investing in securities issued by an affiliate, other than with respect to shares of a subsidiary. See 12 U.S.C. § 1468(a)(1).

Employment Contracts

Federal savings associations are subject to a regulation governing employment contracts. There is no similar regulation for national banks.

Federal Savings Associations - 12 C.F.R. § 163.39

Twelve C.F.R. § 163.39 provides that a savings association may enter into an employment contract with its officers and other employees only in accordance with the requirements of this regulation. All employment contracts must be in writing and approved by the board of directors. A savings association shall not enter into an employment contract with any of its officers or other employees if such contract would constitute an unsafe or unsound practice. The making of such an employment contract would be an unsafe or unsound practice if such contract could lead to material financial loss or damage to the association or could interfere materially with the exercise by the members of its board of directors of their duty or discretion provided by law, charter, bylaw or regulation as to the employment or termination of employment of an officer or employee of the association. This may occur, depending upon the circumstances of the case, where an employment contract provides for an excessive term.

See 12 C.F.R. § 163.39 for list of required provisions that each employment contract must contain.

National Banks

At national banks, employment contract issues are addressed through a safety and soundness analysis. Depending on the circumstances, the provisions of an employment contract may be an unsafe or unsound practice.

Conflicts of Interest

In addition to Regulation O and Regulation W, federal savings associations are subject to a regulation governing conflicts of interest. There is no similar regulation for national banks.[13]

Federal Savings Associations - 12 C.F.R. § 163.200

Directors, officers, employees of federal savings associations, or individuals who have the power to direct its management or policies or otherwise owe a fiduciary duty to the savings association:

- Must not advance their own personal or business interests, or those of others with whom they have a personal or business relationship, at the expense of the savings association; and
- Must, if they have an interest in a matter or transaction before the board of directors:
  - (i)   disclose to the board all material nonprivileged information relevant to the board's decision on the matter or transaction, including the existence, nature and extent of the person's interest and the facts known to the person as to the matter or transaction under consideration;
  - (ii)   refrain from participating in the board's discussion of the matter or transaction; and
  - (iii)   recuse themselves from voting on the matter or transaction (if the person is a director).

National Banks

Although national bank directors and officers are not subject to a regulation regarding conflicts of interest, they do owe a common law fiduciary duty of loyalty to the bank. The duty of loyalty requires directors and management to act in the best interest of the bank and to ensure that insiders do not abuse their positions by benefiting personally at the bank's expense. In general, a conflict of interest exists when the personal or business interests of insiders are inconsistent with the continued safe and sound operation of the bank or with a business opportunity of the institution. Insiders should avoid placing themselves in a position that creates a conflict of interest or the appearance of a conflict of interest. Management and members of the board must fully disclose any personal interest that they have in matters affecting the bank and must ensure that these business and personal relationships with the bank are always at arm's length. Disinterested directors should approve transactions involving the interests of other affiliated parties, and the interested party should abstain from voting and deliberating on any matter

---

[13] But savings association and national bank directors and officers owe a common law fiduciary duty of loyalty to their respective institutions and, of course, are required at all times to maintain and promote the safety and soundness of their financial institution. See heading **Conflicts of Interest - National Banks** in main text for discussion of common law fiduciary duty of loyalty.

involving their own interest. See Comptroller's Handbook, Insider Activities and The Director's Book, published by the OCC.

Usurpation of Corporate Opportunity

Federal savings associations are subject to a regulation governing usurpation of corporate opportunity. There is no similar regulation for national banks.

Federal Savings Associations - 12 C.F.R. § 163.201

Directors, officers, or individuals who have the power to direct its management or policies or otherwise owe a fiduciary duty to the savings association must not take advantage of corporate opportunities belonging to the association. A corporate opportunity belongs to the association if:

- The opportunity is within the corporate powers of the association or a subsidiary of the association; and
- The opportunity is of present or potential practical advantage to the association, either directly or through its subsidiary.

The OCC will not deem an individual to have taken advantage of a corporate opportunity belonging to the association if a disinterested and independent majority of the association's board of directors, after receiving a full and fair presentation of the matter, rejected the opportunity as a matter of sound business judgment.[14]

National Banks

Although national banks directors and officers are not subject to a regulation regarding usurpation of corporate opportunity, they do owe a fiduciary duty of loyalty to the bank (see discussion under heading **Conflicts of Interest**). The "usurpation of corporate opportunity" doctrine, a part of the duty of loyalty, prevents insiders from improperly taking business opportunities away from the bank. See Comptroller's Handbook, Insider Activities and The Director's Book, published by the OCC.

Loan Procurement Fees - 12 C.F.R. § 160.130

Federal savings association directors, officers, or other persons having the power to direct the management or policies of a savings association must not receive, directly or indirectly, any commission, fee, or other compensation in connection with the procurement of any loan made by the savings association or a subsidiary of the savings association.

---

[14] Savings association directors and officers also owe a common law fiduciary duty of loyalty to the savings association. See heading **Conflicts of Interest – National Banks** in main text for discussion of common law fiduciary duty of loyalty.

There is no similar regulation for national banks. Depending on circumstances, the payment of a procurement fee to a national bank director or officer could be an unsafe or unsound practice or a breach of fiduciary duty.

III. CORPORATE GOVERNANCE ISSUES

Indemnification

For administrative proceedings or civil actions initiated by a Federal banking agency, federal savings associations and national banks are subject to the same rule – they may make or agree to make reasonable indemnification payments to an institution-affiliated party ("IAP") [15] only if such payments are consistent with the requirements of 12 C.F.R. § 359.5. [16]

However, as discussed below, there are differences in the rules for federal savings associations and national banks regarding indemnification payments for other types of actions. Please note that for these types of actions, federal savings associations are required to obtain OCC nonobjection before making any indemnification payments - national banks are not required to obtain OCC nonobjection for indemnification payments.

Federal Savings Associations - 12 C.F.R. § 145.121

For actions not initiated by a Federal banking agency, a federal savings association is required to indemnify any person against whom an action is brought or threatened because that person is or was a director, officer, or employee of the association [17] for: (i) any amount for which that person becomes liable under a judgment; and (ii) reasonable costs and expenses, only if final judgment on the merits is in his or her favor. A federal savings association is permitted to indemnify any such person for the amounts described in (i) and (ii) in the previous sentence in the case of settlement, final

---

[15] IAP is defined to include: (i) a director, officer, employee, or controlling stockholder of, or agent for, a bank; (ii) any other person who has filed or is required to file a change-in control notice; (iii) any shareholder, joint venture partner, and any other person who participates in the conduct of the affairs of the bank; and (iv) any independent contractor who knowingly or recklessly participates in certain actions. See 12 U.S.C. § 1813(u) for further detail.

[16] Generally, this regulation provides that an insured depository institution may make or agree to make reasonable indemnification payments to an officer, director, or employee if: (i) the board of directors, in good faith, determines in writing that the person in question acted in good faith and in a manner he/she believed to be in the best interests of the institution; (ii) the board of directors, in good faith, determines in writing that the payment of such expenses will not materially adversely affect the institution's safety and soundness; (iii) the indemnification payments do not constitute "prohibited indemnification payments" under 12 C.F.R. § 359.1(l); and (iv) the person agrees in writing to reimburse the institution, to the extent not covered by payments from insurance or bonds, for that portion of the advances indemnification payments which subsequently become prohibited pursuant to 12 C.F.R. § 359.1(l). See 12 C.F.R. § 359.5 for additional detail.

[17] Note that 12 C.F.R. § 145.121 applies only to officers, directors, and employees, and not to all IAPs.

judgment against him/her, or final judgment in his or her favor other than on the merits, if a majority of the disinterested directors determine that the individual was acting in good faith within the scope of his or her employment or authority as he or she could reasonably have perceived it under the circumstances and for a purpose he or she could reasonably have believed under the circumstances was in the best interests of the association or its members.

In either of the situations described in the previous paragraph, however, no indemnification shall be made unless the federal savings association gives the supervisory office at least *60 days notice* of its intention to make such indemnification. See 12 C.F.R. § 145.121(c) for information that should be included in the notice. *The supervisory office shall promptly acknowledge receipt of the notice and the notice period shall run from the date of such receipt. No such indemnification shall be made if the OCC advises the association in writing within the notice period of its objection to the payment.*

No federal savings association shall indemnify any person covered by this regulation, other than in accordance with this regulation. However, an association which had a bylaw in effect relating to indemnification of its personnel prior to the 1969 implementation date of the indemnification regulation is governed solely by that bylaw.

National Banks - 12 C.F.R. § 7.2014

For administrative proceedings or civil actions not initiated by a Federal banking agency, a national bank may indemnify an IAP for damages and expenses in accordance with the law of the state in which the bank's main office is located, the law of the state where bank's holding company is incorporated, or the relevant provisions of the Model Business Corporation Act, or Delaware General Corporation law, provided the payments are consistent with safe and sound banking practices. A national bank shall designate in its bylaws the body of law selected for making the indemnification payments.

A national bank is not required to obtain OCC non-objection for these indemnification payments.

Board Composition Requirements

Federal Savings Associations - 12 C.F.R. §§ 144.5(b)(8), 152.3, 152.7(b), and 163.33

Federal savings associations are subject to 12 C.F.R. § 163.33, governing composition of the Board of Directors. The regulation provides that composition of the board of directors of a savings association must be in accordance with the following requirements:

- A majority of the directors must not be salaried officers or employees of the savings association or of any subsidiary or any holding company affiliate (except

22

in the case of a savings association having 80% or more of any class of voting shares owned by a holding company).
- Not more than two directors may be members of the same immediate family.
- Not more than one director may be an attorney with a particular law firm.

Additional requirements apply to the composition of the board of a federal savings association, whether in stock or mutual form. The bylaws are required to state a specific number of directors, not a range. This number must be at least five but not more than fifteen. It may exceed fifteen with OCC approval. 12 C.F.R. §§ 144.5(b)(8), 152.3, & 152.7(b).

A federal savings association's board of directors is not subject to citizenship and residence requirements.

The bylaws of a federal mutual savings association must require a president, one or more vice presidents, a secretary, and a treasurer or comptroller. 12 C.F.R. § 144.5(b)(10).

National Banks – 12 U.S.C. §§ 71a, 72, & 76, 12 C.F.R. § 7.2012

No regulation similar to 12 C.F.R. § 163.33 applies to national banks. However, citizenship and residence requirements apply to a national bank's board of directors. 12 U.S.C. § 72.

Statutory requirements govern the number of directors of a national bank. The board must have at least five but not more than 25 members. The OCC may permit more than 25 members by order or regulation. 12 U.S.C. § 71a.

In addition, the president (but not the chief executive officer) of the bank is required to be a member of the board. The board may elect a director other than the president to be chairman of the board. 12 U.S.C. § 76; 12 C.F.R. § 7.2012.

Qualifying Shares or Membership

National banks and federal savings associations are subject to different rules regarding whether directors are required to own an equity interest in the financial institutions.

Federal Savings Associations - 12 C.F.R. §§ 152.7 (stock) and 144.5(b)(8) (mutual)

A director of a federal stock savings association need not be a stockholder of the association unless the bylaws so require. A director of a federal mutual savings association must be a member of the association.

National Banks - 12 C.F.R. § 7.2005

A national bank director must own a qualifying equity interest in a national bank or a company that has control of a national bank. The director must own the qualifying equity interest in his or her own right and meet a certain minimum threshold ownership. See 12 C.F.R. § 7.2005 for details as to the types of ownership that satisfies the requirement of this section.

Corporate Title

There is no requirement for the name of a federal savings association other than a federal savings association shall not adopt a title that misrepresents the nature of the institution or the services it offers. 12 C.F.R. § 143.1. The federal savings association must provide notice to OCC of a change in title, and OCC has *30 days* to object to the change.

The name of a national bank must include the word "national." 12 U.S.C. § 22. A national bank may change its corporate title provided that the new title includes the word "national" and complies with other applicable Federal laws and any applicable OCC guidance. A national bank shall promptly notify the appropriate district office if it changes its corporate title. The notice must contain the old and new titles and the effective date of the change. 12 U.S.C. § 30 and 12 C.F.R. § 5.42.

IV. SUBSIDIARIES AND NON-CONTROLLING INVESTMENTS

Federal savings associations are authorized to invest in operating subsidiaries, bank service companies,[18] service corporations, and pass-through investments. National banks are authorized to invest in operating subsidiaries, bank service companies, financial subsidiaries, and noncontrolling investments.

Operating Subsidiaries

Federal savings associations and national banks are both authorized to invest in operating subsidiaries.

---

[18]   It appears that OTS has not used the authority under the Bank Service Company Act to address a federal savings association's investment in a bank service company. Instead, depending on the ownership interest and the activities to be conducted, associations have made such investments pursuant to the operating subsidiary provisions in 12 C.F.R. Part 159, the pass-through investment provisions of 12 C.F.R. § 160.32, or the service corporation provisions in 12 C.F.R. Part 159.

Federal Savings Associations - 12 C.F.R. Part 159

A Federal savings association operating subsidiary may engage in any activity that the savings association may conduct directly.[19]

- The savings association must own, directly or indirectly, more than 50% of the voting shares of the operating subsidiary. No one else may exercise effective operating control; and
- The savings association and its operating subsidiary are generally consolidated and treated as a unit for statutory and regulatory purposes.

Please refer to 12 C.F.R. Parts 159 and 116 for additional detail and for information on notice and application filing requirements.

National Banks - 12 C.F.R. § 5.34

A national bank operating subsidiary may engage in activities that are permissible for a national bank to engage in directly either as part of, or incidental to, the business of banking, as determined by the OCC, or otherwise under other statutory authority.[20]

An operating subsidiary in which a national bank may invest includes a corporation, limited liability company, limited partnership, or similar entity if:

- The bank has the ability to control the management and operations of the subsidiary;
- The parent bank owns and controls more than 50% of the voting (or similar type of controlling) interest of the operating subsidiary, or the parent bank otherwise controls the operating subsidiary and no other party controls more than 50% of the voting (or similar type of controlling) interest of the operating subsidiary; and
- the operating subsidiary is consolidated with the bank under GAAP.

Please refer to 12 C.F.R. § 5.34 for additional detail and for information on notice and application filing requirements.

---

[19] Because there are differences in the activities that national banks and federal savings associations may engage in directly, the permissible activities of their operating subsidiaries may also differ.
[20] See footnote 19.

<u>Bank Service Companies</u> - <u>12 U.S.C. §§ 1861-1867</u> and <u>12 C.F.R. § 5.35</u>

National banks and federal savings associations are both authorized to invest in bank service companies under the Bank Service Company Act, <u>12 U.S.C. § 1861 *et. seq*</u>.

- A bank service company is any corporation or limited liability company organized to provide services authorized by the Bank Service Company Act.[21]
    - If the bank service company is a corporation, all of the capital stock must be owned by one or more insured depository institutions.
    - If the bank service company is a limited liability company ("LLC"), all of the members of the LLC must be one or more insured depository institutions.
- A bank or saving association may not invest more than 10% of its capital and surplus in a bank service company. In addition, a bank's or association's total investments in all bank service companies may not exceed 5% of the bank's or association's total assets.[22]

There is no regulation that governs a federal savings association's investment in a bank service company.[23]

A national bank that wants to invest in a bank service company must comply with the requirements of <u>12 C.F.R. § 5.35</u>.

<u>Service Corporations</u> - <u>12 C.F.R. Part 159</u>

Federal savings associations are authorized to invest in service corporations; national banks are not authorized to invest in them.

A service corporation is any entity that satisfies all the requirements in <u>12 U.S.C. § 1464(c)(4)(B)</u> and <u>12 C.F.R. § 159.3</u>.

- A federal savings association is not required to have any particular percentage ownership interest in a service corporation and does not need to have control of the service corporation.
- A service corporation must be organized in the state where the association's home office is located and may only be owned by associations with home offices in that

---

[21] Authorized activities include providing the following services only for depository institutions: check and deposit posting and sorting; computation and posting of interest and other credits and charges; preparation and mailing of checks, statements, notices, and similar items; or any other clerical, bookkeeping, accounting, statistical, or similar function. Bank service companies are also authorized to perform such services (other than taking deposits) that each depository institution shareholder or member is otherwise authorized to perform under any applicable Federal or state law, but may only perform such services at locations in a State in which each shareholder or member is authorized to perform such services.
[22] But see <u>12 U.S.C. § 1862</u> which appears to limit a savings association's investment in a bank service company to either 2% or 3% of assets. This issue is unresolved pending future rule-making by the OCC.
[23] See footnote 18.

- A service corporation may invest in all types of lower-tier entities as long as the lower-tier entity is engaged solely in activities that are permissible for a service corporation.[24]
- Generally, an association may invest up to 3% of its assets in the capital stock, obligations, and other securities of service corporations. Any investment that would cause the association's investment, in the aggregate, to exceed 2% the association's assets must serve primarily community, inner city, or community development purposes. See 12 C.F.R. § 159.5 for additional detail on investment authority and how investment is treated under lending limit rules.
- If the association is eligible for expedited treatment,[25] and files a *30 day prior notice* with its appropriate Licensing office, the service corporation may engage in the preapproved activities listed in 12 C.F.R. § 159.4.[26] The association may also request OCC approval for the service corporation to engage in any other activity reasonably related to the activities of financial institutions by filing an application with its appropriate Licensing office in accordance with standard treatment processing procedures found at 12 C.F.R. Part 116, subparts A and E.
- If the association is eligible for standard treatment,[27] and files a *30 day prior notice* with its appropriate Licensing office, the service corporation may engage in any activity that the association may conduct directly, except taking deposits.[28] The association may also request OCC approval for the service corporation to engage in any other activity reasonably related to the activities of financial institutions by filing an application with its appropriate Licensing office in accordance with standard treatment processing procedures found at 12 C.F.R. Part 116, subparts A and E.
- The capital treatment of a service corporation depends upon whether it is an includable subsidiary – see 12 C.F.R. Part 167 for detail.

Financial Subsidiaries - 12 C.F.R. § 5.39

National banks are authorized to invest in financial subsidiaries; federal savings associations are not authorized to invest in them.

A financial subsidiary is any company that is controlled by one or more insured depository institutions and engages in activities that are financial in nature and activities incidental to a financial activity, authorized pursuant to 12 U.S.C. § 24a. See also

---

[24] See 12 C.F.R. § 159.4 for a list of preapproved activities for a service corporation.

[25] See footnote 3 for explanation of "expedited treatment."

[26] If the notice presents supervisory concerns or raises significant issues of law or policy, the association must apply for and receive OCC approval under standard treatment processing procedures found at 12 C.F.R. Part 116, subparts A and E. See 12 C.F.R. § 159.11.

[27] See footnote 3 for explanation of "standard treatment."

[28] If the notice presents supervisory concerns or raises significant issues of law or policy, the association must apply for and receive OCC approval under standard treatment processing procedures found at 12 C.F.R. Part 116, subparts A and E. See 12 C.F.R. § 159.11.

12 C.F.R. § 5.39. A financial subsidiary needs to engage in at least one activity that is not permissible for the bank to conduct directly.

A national bank may hold an interest in a financial subsidiary only if:

- The national bank and all depository institution affiliates are well-managed and well-capitalized;
- The aggregate consolidated assets of all of a bank's financial subsidiaries do not exceed 45% of the parent bank's consolidated total assets, or $50 billion, whichever is less;
- If the national bank is one of the 50 largest insured banks, the bank has long-term, unsecured debt rated in the top three investment grades, or, if the bank is between 51 to 100 of the largest insure banks, the bank has long-term, unsecured debt rated in the top three investment grades or meets comparable standards; and
- The parent national bank and any insured depository institution affiliate have at least a "satisfactory" CRA rating.

The national bank must deduct its investment in financial subsidiaries from its total assets and tangible equity and from its total risked-based capital. The national bank may not consolidate the assets and liabilities of a financial subsidiary with those of the bank.

There are consequences to national banks who fail to continue to meet the qualification requirements – see 12 C.F.R. § 5.39(j) for additional detail.

Pass-Through Investments/Noncontrolling Investments

A savings association may make pass-through investments. In comparison, national banks may make noncontrolling investments.

Federal Savings Associations - 12 C.F.R. § 160.32

A pass-through investment occurs when an association invests in a company that engages only in activities that the association may conduct directly and that meets the requirements of 12 C.F.R. § 160.32.

A federal savings association may make a pass-through investment without prior notice to OCC if all of the following conditions are met:

- The association does not invest more than 15% of its total capital in one company;
- The book value of the association's aggregate pass-through investments do not exceed 50% of the association's total capital after making the investment;
- The association's investment would not give it direct or indirect control of the company;
- The association's liability is limited to the amount of its investment; and

- The company falls into one of the following categories:
  - a limited partnership;
  - an open-end mutual fund;
  - a closed-end investment trust;
  - a limited liability company; or
  - an entity in which the association is investing primarily to use the company's services (*e.g.* data processing).

To make a pass-through investment that does not meet the conditions listed above, the savings association must file a ***30-days' advance notice*** with its appropriate Licensing office. If within the 30-day period, OCC notifies the association that the investment presents supervisory, legal, or safety and soundness concerns, the association must file an application with its appropriate Licensing office and receive prior written approval before making the investment.[29]

National Banks - 12 C.F.R. § 5.36

A national bank may make a noncontrolling investment, directly or through its operating subsidiary, in an enterprise[30] that engages in the following activities:

- Activities described at 12 C.F.R. § 5.34(e)(5)(v);[31] or
- Activities that are substantially the same as that contained in published OCC precedent approving a noncontrolling investment by a national bank or operating subsidiary.[32]

Before making a noncontrolling investment, a bank must satisfy the following requirements:

- The bank must be able to prevent the enterprise from engaging in activities that are not set forth in 12 C.F.R. § 5.34(e)(5)(v) or not contained in published OCC precedent - otherwise, the bank must have the ability to withdraw its investment from the enterprise;

---

[29] The application must be filed under the standard treatment processing procedures at 12 C.F.R. Part 116, subparts A and E. Once the application is deemed complete, the OCC has ***60 days*** to review it and render a decision. ***If the OCC fails to act within the 60-day period, the application is deemed to be automatically approved.***

[30] An "enterprise" means any corporation, limited liability company, partnership, trust, or similar business entity. See 12 C.F.R. § 5.36(c)(1).

[31] This regulation describes the preapproved activities for an operating subsidiary and includes activities such as making loans or other extensions of credit; selling money orders, savings bonds, and travelers checks; purchasing, selling, servicing, or warehousing loans; providing courier services between financial institutions; providing check guaranty, verification, and payment services; providing data processing for the bank or its affiliates; providing tax planning and preparation services; providing financial and transaction advice and assistance; etc. See 12 C.F.R. § 5.34(e)(5)(v) for complete list of activities.

[32] The activities must be conducted according to the same terms and conditions applicable to the activities covered by the precedent and the national bank must provide the applicable cite to the precedent.

- Investment must be convenient and useful to the bank in carrying out its business and not merely a passive investment;
- The bank's loss exposure must be limited as a legal matter; and
- The enterprise in which the bank is investing must agree to be subject to OCC supervision and examination, subject to functional regulation limitations.

See 12 C.F.R. § 5.36 for additional detail on noncontrolling investments and for information on notice/application filing requirements.[33]

Separate Corporate Identities – 12 C.F.R. § 159.10

Federal savings associations are subject to a regulation governing separate corporate identities. There is no similar regulation for national banks.

Each savings association and operating subsidiary, service corporation or lower-tier entity must be operated in a manner that demonstrates to the public that each maintains a separate corporate existence. Each must operate so that:

- Their respective business transactions, accounts, and records are not intermingled;
- Each observes the formalities of their separate corporate procedures;
- Each is adequately financed as a separate unit in light of normal obligations reasonably foreseeable in a business of its size and character;
- Each is held out to the public as a separate enterprise; and
- Unless the parent savings association has guaranteed a loan to the entity, all borrowings by the entity indicate that the savings association is not liable.

At national banks, corporate separability issues are addressed through a safety and soundness analysis.

---

[33] Please note that it is possible that a national bank and a federal savings association investing in the same company may have different filing requirements with the OCC. Consider, for example, the situation where a bank and an association both own a participation interest in the same REO and both entities want to exchange their REO interest for an equivalent interest in an LLC that would hold, manage, and dispose of the property. The savings association would not be required to file any notice or application with the OCC, provided the savings association could dispose of its investment in 5 years (REO holding period) and could otherwise satisfy the requirements of 12 C.F.R. § 160.32. In contrast, a national bank would need to file with the OCC either the notice required by Interpretive Letter #1123 or the notice or application required by 12 C.F.R. § 5.36(e), (f), or (g).

www.ingramcontent.com/pod-product-compliance
Lightning Source LLC
Chambersburg PA
CBHW080737290526
45790CB00008B/3236